PUFFIN BOOKS

PLAYING WITH FIRE

What on earth seems to be the matter with the staff of St Elmer's Primary School? They say it's freezing when it's warm, make up new school rules on the spot, and generally act quite out of character. There is something very mysterious going on. Could it have anything to do with the legend of the masked monks and their stolen treasure, buried on the ancient abbey site where the new school is built? Chris and Tim decide to find out, and they're in for some alarming surprises.

This is an original, funny story in which the pupils must battle to outwit their teachers if the school is to survive.

Anthony Masters is the author of numerous books for children and also writes for adults. He has run drama workshops and is a regular writer-in-residence in schools and colleges. He is married with three children and lives in East Sussex.

ANTHONY MASTERS

Playing with Fire

Illustrated by John Levers

PUFFIN BOOKS
in association with
Blackie and Son Limited

To Melissa
the original Miss Holroyd

PUFFIN BOOKS

Published by the Penguin Group
Penguin Books Ltd, 27 Wrights Lane, London W8 5TZ, England
Penguin Books USA Inc., 375 Hudson Street, New York, New York 10014, USA
Penguin Books Australia Ltd, Ringwood, Victoria, Australia
Penguin Books Canada Ltd, 10 Alcorn Avenue, Toronto, Ontario, Canada M4V 3B2
Penguin Books (NZ) Ltd, 182–190 Wairau Road, Auckland 10, New Zealand

Penguin Books Ltd, Registered Offices: Harmondsworth, Middlesex, England

First published by Blackie and Son Ltd 1990
Published in Puffin Books 1992
1 3 5 7 9 10 8 6 4 2

1 . . .

The September sky was black and stormy and it was very hot. Tim sat eating his breakfast, feeling excited. His school had just moved into a brand new building and he wondered what it was going to be like. Would the teachers be any different in a new place, or would they be their same old selves?

Dad was just going off to work. He was in one of his jolly teasing moods, which Tim knew always got on Mum's nerves, particularly in the early morning.

'Well, me old son, off to school with all those old spooks, are you?' He burst into hearty laughter. 'Wonder what it'll be like, doing maths with a masked monk? Bet he'll be good at money sums, anyway!'

'Do shut up,' said Mum. 'You're wearing that joke to death.'

Dad grabbed Tim's school sweater and quickly threw it over Tim's head. 'You'll soon be a masked monk yourself,' he said. 'When do they

let you into the gang? At assembly?'

Mum groaned as Tim's head popped out of the sweater. 'Now look what you've done,' she said furiously. 'You've spilt the milk.'

'It's a magic sign,' said Dad, grabbing his cap and hurrying out of the room.

Tim looked ruefully at the table-cloth. What a mess, he thought. Dad and his stupid jokes. The spilt milk had spread into one large shape and it looked like a swollen cloud.

* * *

6

The sky was so dark that it was almost like night. Tim and Chris watched out of the windows of the school bus. They had never seen anything like it in their lives. The clouds were a very dark purple, and they looked as if they were bulging. Suddenly a snaked fork of lightning tore the air in a crackle of jagged blue.

'You know what?' exclaimed Chris. 'That came from the ground, not the air!'

'Couldn't have done.'

The bus had just stopped outside the new St Elmer's Primary School and as the children poured out, Mr Ransom, the school bus driver, said kindly: 'Keep close to Mrs Edge. She's here to help you across the road as usual.'

'My bag!' said Tim. 'Hang on a minute, Chris. I've left it on the back seat.'

'Buck up,' said Chris impatiently.

More lightning crackled and flashed as the two boys ran across the playground towards the shiny new building. Still no rain came. Then they heard the unfamiliar sound of an electronic school bell bleeping away, and saw the deputy head, Miss Holroyd, standing on the steps. She was short and dumpy and just a little more flustered than usual.

'Come on, you two,' she wailed. 'You don't

want to be struck by lightning, do you? Not on your first day in our new school.'

Miss Sands, the headmistress, was Tim and Chris's form teacher. She was immensely fat with several quivering chins, but although her appearance was a continuous joke, the children were fond of her. She was strong on discipline but had a good sense of humour and her lessons were rarely dull.

Now Miss Sands was asking why Billy Pierce had not done his homework. Because he wasn't

telling her she was getting more and more annoyed, so Tim and Chris were able to talk in whispers. They had been friends since the reception class, and relied on each other a good deal.

'What do you think of the place then?' asked Chris.

'It's OK. I expect we'll soon get used to it.' There was a pause. Then Tim added sadly: 'Hope it's break soon. I had an awful breakfast.'

'Your dad been going on again?' asked Chris.

Tim told him and Chris shook with suppressed laughter. 'Well, the legend could be true, you know,' he whispered. 'The local paper had a bit on it. Didn't you see it?'

'No. Never read the paper. I'd rather read the *Beano*.'

'I cut it out for you.' Chris passed Tim a screwed up bit of paper. He unfolded it and read:

SCHOOL OPENS ON BLACK ABBEY SITE

STUPID SUPERSTITION, SAYS HEAD TEACHER

The new St Elmer's Primary School opens on Monday on land that has remained derelict since the eleventh century. Until now, local superstition has always prevented the land from being used. Legend has it that there was once a small abbey on the site and that the last four monks to live there forgot their vows and began to rob the local community. They were thought to have amassed a fortune before the abbey was struck by lightning and burnt to the ground. The Masked Monks, as they were known, perished in the flames, but it has always been suspected that the treasure survived as the monks were reputed to have hidden it down a well. Over the centuries many searches for the well have been recorded, and as recently as 1982 . . .

Tim gave Chris back his crumpled newspaper cutting without bothering to read on. 'Lot of old rubbish,' he declared.

'Supposing it's true?' asked Chris, looking disappointed.

'Well, it's not. You're as bad as my dad.'

'Be quiet!' Miss Sands said firmly. 'Go and sit down, Billy Pierce, and don't try to get round me.'

Grimacing, Billy returned to his desk as Miss Sands turned to the rest of the class.

'Settle down now. You may be in a new building, but I can assure you we're all going to behave in exactly the same old way.'

The storm was making a terrific noise outside the assembly hall as they tried to sing a hymn. Miss Sands, crouched low over the piano, was bashing out the chords as if her life depended on it. She was in competition with the noise outside, and as she entered the second verse the rain started to lash down really hard. Smiling at the children reassuringly, she continued to play until there was a sharp clap of thunder immediately overhead. Then suddenly, to everyone's astonishment, she began to play faster and faster.

Chris looked at the sides of the hall where the other staff were standing. They all looked puzzled but no one did anything. Instead, like the children, they sang faster and faster until the hymn was going at breakneck speed.

On the last line another tremendously loud clap of thunder cracked out above them and Miss Sands came to a grinding halt. She slammed down the piano lid and stood up. There was complete silence as she gazed at them all in distress.

'It's too cold,' she said suddenly. 'Far too cold.'

'What do you mean?' asked Miss Holroyd. 'Where is it too cold?'

As she spoke the thunder roared again and the door at the back opened. Through it ran the caretaker, Mr Miles, the lollipop lady, Mrs Edge, and the school bus driver, Mr Ransom.

'I'm sorry to interrupt assembly, Miss Sands, but the place is freezing.' Mr Miles looked round at the pupils. 'We'll have complaints from the parents.'

11

Mrs Edge, the lollipop lady, was usually full of bouncy jokes but this time her teeth were chattering. 'It's all over the school,' she said. 'I've never been so cold.'

'It's not right for the kids,' Mr Ransom added. He shivered and it seemed as if his whole thin body was trembling.

'What on earth's the matter with them all?' whispered Chris. 'It's really warm in here.'

Tim shook his head. 'I don't know. Perhaps it is a bit chilly. I expect they just want to get it right for us.'

'Fancy breaking into assembly like this,' said Chris. 'Miss Sands would've been furious in the old school. And why was she playing so fast?'

Miss Sands put up a hand, stopping Mrs Edge from bubbling more complaints at her. 'There's only one thing for it,' she said. 'Mr Miles, you must investigate the central heating system more closely. Meanwhile, we shall all do physical exercises.' Miss Sands stood, arms outstretched. 'Stand up everybody,' she commanded. As they shuffled to their feet, she began to jump up and down, her arms and legs stretched wide. 'One and two,' she cried. 'One and two. One and two. Come on, everybody. Stretch upwards. We'll soon

12

get warm.'

'I'm sweating,' panted Chris, but when he glanced at Tim he was dutifully following Miss Sands, who looked like a dancing elephant. Miss Holroyd was staring at her with a mixture of anxiety and despair. Then she rushed to her side and gripped her arm.

'Emily! You are not yourself.'

There was an exhausted silence and a few nervous giggles as Miss Sands stopped the physical jerks and turned to Miss Holroyd.

'I am needed,' she gasped. 'You will find me – in the boiler-house.'

'Is something wrong there?' Miss Holroyd looked totally bewildered.

'Wrong?' snapped Miss Sands. 'Certainly not *wrong*.' She turned to Mrs Edge and Mr Ransom. Mr Miles had already gone. 'Come, we are needed.' And with that she strode out, her black shoes rapping on the floor.

Tim had often wondered what a stunned silence was really like and now he knew. Everyone simply stared at each other, and no one said anything at all for a very long time. Then the buzz of amazement began. It increased while the teachers talked amongst themselves, but none of them seemed able to decide what should be done. For a while Miss Holroyd stood alone on the stage, turning her head this way and that. She reminded Tim of an old hen looking for her chicks. Then she raised a hand for silence and teachers and pupils stopped talking at once.

'Boys and girls,' said Miss Holroyd slowly. 'As you know, Miss Sands is most concerned about the central heating and in her usual practical way has helped us all – to warm up.' She was still panting a little from her own forced exercise. 'She will return shortly. In the meantime you will all go quietly to your classes and get on with your work. You are dismissed.'

As Miss Sands was their teacher, Chris and Tim were looking forward to a free period, but after five minutes or so Miss Holroyd arrived. She set them some work and then sat staring out of the window. She drummed her fingers on the desk, and took no notice of them at all.

'Please, miss.'

'Yes, Chris?'

'Shall I go and look for Miss Sands?'

'Certainly not. She is very busy. Get on with

your work.'

'Please, miss?' asked Chris again.

'Yes?' She looked at him warily.

'What do you think Miss Sands is doing in the boiler-house?'

'I've just said,' she rapped out as a snigger went up. 'She's very busy. No more questions.'

At eleven the bell rang and they all went out into the playground. The boiler-house was down the far end and, slowly but surely, the whole school began to drift down towards it.

'What are they doing in there?' asked Amanda Scott, who was a very managing sort of girl.

'Search me,' said Chris.

'Don't you think we should take a look?'

'Yeah,' said her constant companion Shirley. 'Why don't you take a look?'

'I think we should leave them alone,' said Tim. 'It's none of our business.'

Chris and Amanda looked at each other.

'You going in?' she asked.

'All right.'

'We could get into trouble—' began Tim.

'Chicken,' said Amanda and Shirley grinned.

'We could go in together. Pretend we're worried

about her. And the others,' Chris said.

'All right,' replied Amanda. 'Why not?'

Shirley and Tim exchanged doubtful looks. This would definitely end in trouble. Big trouble.

Watched by a hundred pairs of fascinated eyes, Chris and Amanda began to walk slowly towards the boiler-house. They were both nervous, but were determined not to show it.

'Don't go in,' snapped Tim. 'She'll be furious.'

His words speeded them up, however, and they began to run, arriving at the entrance to the boiler-house together.

'After you,' said Amanda.

'Why not after you?' muttered Chris as he stumbled on. They disappeared inside the doorway and there was a long silence while the curiosity of the other children rose to unbearable heights. Tim gazed anxiously at the boiler-house door, but soon, out of the corner of his eye, he saw that the other teachers were walking towards them with Miss Holroyd at the front.

'Just what's going on here?' she asked.

'They've gone in to see if they can help,' said Tim.

Immediately she was angry. 'How dare they

interfere?' She paused and then steeled herself. 'I shall go and fetch them out. I'm sure Miss Sands has everything well under control.' She moved forward authoritatively and opened the boiler-house door.

Directly they opened the door, Chris and Amanda were almost driven back by an intense heat. It was so strong that they could hardly bear it. At first they couldn't make out anything at all as the room was filled with a kind of red mist. Then it cleared, but the room felt as hot as the sauna that Chris had once been to with his dad.

'Look,' said Amanda. She gripped his arm so fiercely that it hurt.

'Blimey,' said Chris. 'What *do* they think they're doing?'

Miss Sands, Mr Ransom and Mrs Edge were on their knees. In front of them roared the flames of an open boiler. 'I thought it was oil-fired central heating,' hissed Amanda. 'It was at the old school.'

It was odd, thought Chris, to have an old-fashioned boiler, roaring with flames like this, in a brand new school. And what on earth were they all doing?

'There's something in the flames,' whispered Amanda. 'Look, it's a demon. A real demon!'

'A what?'

But it was, a little red demon, sitting on the red hot coal. He looked quite comfortable.

'Isn't he sweet?' said Amanda. She didn't seem in the least scared.

'Sweet? Him?' Chris stared at the demon goggle-eyed.

There was a shrill scream and like a flash they both turned round. Miss Holroyd was standing just behind them.

Tim thought that the silence would go on forever. He glanced at Shirley, but she was staring straight ahead. The thunder was still growling in the distance, but the rain and the lightning had stopped.

Without warning, the boiler-house door burst open and Miss Holroyd came running out, still screaming. Behind her came Chris and Amanda. Amanda was very red in the face and Chris was very pale. What on earth could have happened? wondered Tim. Miss Holroyd rushed sobbing into the arms of the Lower Juniors' teacher, Mr Bunker. Meanwhile Amanda, cheeks flushed even more brightly, stood with Chris a few yards away.

'Well?' asked Tim, unable to bear it any longer. 'What are they up to?'

'It was amazing,' said Chris. But then he stopped. It was as if a dark blanket had been placed over his memory. He looked at Amanda helplessly, wondering if the same thing had happened to her.

'Well?' Tim was impatient.

'I can't remember,' Chris muttered. He wondered for a moment if he was going mad. Then he heard Miss Holroyd saying the same words over and over again.

'I can't remember anything, George. I just can't remember a thing.'

'Here they come,' said Tim in a very level voice. 'They look fine, don't they?'

They certainly did. Miss Sands, Mrs Edge, Mr Miles and Mr Ransom looked very much their ordinary selves as they came out of the boiler-house. Miss Sands drew herself up to her full height.

'The problem is resolved, children. Thanks to the expertise of Mr Miles, the heating system is now working properly.'

'If only I could remember what happened in there,' said Chris to Amanda. 'Can't *you* remember anything?'

'Nothing.'

He turned to Tim. 'Don't you think Miss Sands seems pretty odd?'

'No,' said Tim abruptly. 'She's perfectly normal – like all the others.'

Perhaps they are, thought Chris, disappointed.

The next morning Chris and Tim were waiting at the top end of their estate for the school bus. It was a blustery day and the sun looked like a tired orange in the sky. They saw the bus in the distance. It was racing along much faster than usual, and there was a plume of spray surrounding it, for it had continued to rain hard last night.

It eventually roared up in front of them and stopped with a screech of brakes. Amanda and Shirley and Billy Pierce were sitting at the back. There was something wrong with them. They looked cowed and frightened. Hurriedly Chris and Tim leapt up the steps and came face to face with Mr Ransom. His bald head was very shiny and his long narrow face looked as if it had been made up with chalk. There was definitely something different about him. He always did look thin and pale but today his face was dead white.

'Stop,' said Mr Ransom in a flat sort of voice.

'Yes?' Chris stared at him in surprise.

'No running.'

'Eh?'

'No running on to the bus.'

'Oh.'

Tim belted up the steps behind Chris and said: 'What's that?'

'No running on to the bus,' repeated Mr Ransom's flat voice. 'And no talking either.'

'No talking? This isn't school.' For once Tim was angry.

'You want to argue with me?' asked Mr Ransom in his new unfriendly way.

'No,' said Chris hastily. 'I don't want to argue.'

'Then go and sit down. And not another word from either of you. Do you understand?'

'Yes,' said Tim. 'We understand.'

They walked slowly to the back of the bus, passing rows of subdued and miserable-looking children. They sat down next to Amanda and Shirley and Billy.

'Is he barmy?' whispered Chris to Billy. But before Billy could whisper back a voice hissed down the bus: 'I said no talking.'

'How did he hear that?' asked Chris and Amanda gave him a pleading look.

'Right,' said Mr Ransom. 'You will go to Miss Sands directly you arrive at school.' He looked very cross indeed.

Tim nudged Chris and put a finger to his lips, but even Chris realised that he had better not say any more.

The bus drew up opposite the school and they all had to wait until Mrs Edge, the lollipop lady, came to see them across the road. It had been difficult enough yesterday with the thunderstorm, but this time they were a very subdued group indeed. They had sat silently and fearfully while Mr Ransom had taken them at a furiously jerky pace, and now they were all feeling rather sick.

Mrs Edge crossed the road and greeted them with her usual enthusiasm. She was small and bird-like and was always chattering, but the children enjoyed her predictable jokes and always felt safe crossing the road with her.

'You all look so miserable,' she said, with a piercing shriek of laughter. 'Why don't you cheer up? Look at me – I'm always merry and bright.' She burst out laughing again. 'A little legacy can be a great boost.'

Chris gazed from her to Mr Ransom and noticed that Mr Ransom was giving Mrs Edge a sort of warning look. Whatever is the matter with them both? he wondered.

'Oh, don't mind me. You know I crack a joke a minute,' said Mrs Edge and her piercing laugh rang out again.

I know she does, thought Chris. But not usually quite like this.

As they hurried into the cloakroom they found their way blocked by Miss Sands.

'Chris Elliott.'

'Yes?' He looked up at her fearfully, which was most unlike him.

'I gather you were misbehaving on the bus.'

'I only spoke.'

'That is *not* allowed.'

'But we've *always* been allowed to talk on the bus. It's free time.'

'It is no *longer* free time.'

'Please, Miss Sands,' said Tim.

'Yes?' She looked down at him coldly.

'I don't think it's fair, miss.'

'You *what*?'

'I don't think it's fair.'

'How dare you answer me back? You will both stay in during break and write out "I must do as I'm told" a hundred times.' With that she turned on her heel and lumbered away, looking like an enormous sailing ship pulling through some rough weather.

'That's odd,' said Chris.

'What's odd?'

'Well, Mr Ransom got back in his bus, didn't he? He couldn't have told her about us.'

'No. Then *how* did she know?' said Tim blankly.

'That's the point,' said Chris.

Assembly that morning seemed unusually tense. Miss Holroyd stood on the platform, nervous and very ill at ease. Next to her stood Miss Sands, looking quite stern, but at least the other teachers sat with their classes as usual.

'Let me come straight to the point,' said Miss Sands. 'I want to improve the standard of behaviour, not only in the school but in the playground and on the bus. I shall expect a lot of you.' She cleared her throat warningly as a groan went up from the children. 'We also have a new school project. I shall be sending notes home to your parents about it. I am sure they will be very pleased indeed. For a start, instead of your normal time-table today we are going to organise work parties to clear up the school.'

There was a howl of protest and Miss Sands looked annoyed.

'Yes, we are going to organise a Do-It-Yourself beauty scheme for the school and its grounds. Unfortunately the workmen have left a lot of rubble about and the place still looks a mess. You will all be divided into groups and we will soon have everything in apple pie order.' She moved back and gestured Miss Holroyd forward with beaming firmness.

'There you are, children,' said Miss Holroyd brightly. 'What a wonderful idea.'

There were no lessons that morning. Instead the children were divided into groups and a huge plan of the school was drawn up on one of the boards. It had six areas on it and each was given a work party. Chris and Tim were pleased to find that they were in the same group. They had long ago decided that the only really good thing about school was the football team and Chris in particular was often in trouble for messing about in class. Tim was more attentive and Chris's parents thought he was a good influence on their over-active son. Tim's parents were not so sure and were always asking for them to be split up.

'It's strange, isn't it?' said Chris thoughtfully.

'Strange?' asked Tim.

'They seem to have changed overnight.'

'Who?'

'Sands and Edge and Ransom.'

'In what way?' said Tim scoffingly.

'Something happened in the boiler-house,' replied Chris, 'and I can't remember what it was.'

'*Nothing* happened,' said Tim. 'It can't have. You'd have said.'

'So why can't I remember? Why can't I remember *anything*?'

'I don't know.' Tim was impatient. 'You just forgot, that's all.'

'You don't think it's all true?'

'*What's* all true?'

'The Masked Monks and the treasure in the well.'

'It's just an old story.'

'Suppose the monks have taken over Miss Sands – and the others?'

Tim laughed. 'I can't see Mrs Edge as a Masked Monk, though now you mention it Miss Sands does look a bit like Friar Tuck!'

But Chris was hardly listening. 'They might be working inside them, making them find the treasure. All this clearing out. P'raps they're looking for the well?'

Tim laughed again but this time Chris was annoyed.

'Laugh again and I'll thump you.'

Tim hesitated. Chris in a rage was quite something. He decided to be more tactful. 'You don't have to be so cross,' he said quietly.

'Sorry,' said Chris quickly. 'But don't you think they're behaving in a funny way?'

'No. Sands is tightening up on discipline, that's all. Now we're in a new building. I think the bus is unfair though—' He paused wistfully. 'By the way – I found this. Forgot to tell you in all the commotion.'

'What is it?' Chris stared at the small black object doubtfully.

'It's a key – or what's left of one. The top's gone but the teeth are all intact.'

'Where did you find it?'

'Amongst all that old builders' rubble that's

still down by the bike sheds.'

'What are you going to do with it?' asked Chris, his excitement returning.

'Give it in of course,' said Tim. 'I should have handed it over already.'

'Well, it might be – valuable or something,' replied Chris feebly.

'Exactly why I should give it in,' said Tim in a prim voice.

'You do everything right, don't you?'

'I try to,' said Tim irritatingly.

There were no lessons for anyone all the rest of the day. The group to which Tim and Chris were attached cleared up the assembly hall. They were led by Mr Miles, who gave short, sharp commands in his deep growling voice.

'I want everything under this stage dragged out. Don't leave anything in there at all.'

The builders had left old sandbags, bricks and rubble. It was a tough job but eventually they had cleared everything out until there was nothing underneath the stage but a deep, dark space. Even so, Mr Miles crawled in with a torch and spade. He stayed under the stage for a very long time.

'What's he doing?' asked Jack Boyle.

'Be quiet,' said Mr Wenlock, whose special interest was games. 'Mr Miles knows what he's doing.'

'He's digging,' said Chris. 'What for?'

There was a long silence. 'He's having a look,' replied Mr Wenlock. He sounded doubtful. 'He's having a look – to see if there's any more junk.'

'There's nothing to look *at*,' said Chris. 'We've cleared everything out. But now he's digging up the—'

'Don't be cheeky.'

'I'm just saying—'

'Be quiet at once.' Mr Wenlock turned to shout at the rest of the group. 'All of you – be quiet.'

'You know what—' whispered Chris to Tim. 'It's more like Miles is searching for something – something like a well – and using us as slaves.'

Eventually Mr Miles staggered out, his tufts of red hair standing up, covered in dust and cob-webs, and his shoes caked in earth. He didn't look in the best of moods.

'You've done a fine job there,' he snarled. 'Now we'll start on the sports store. They've left a pile of old bricks in there and more sandbags.'

'What a good idea,' beamed Mr Wenlock. 'I want to move my stuff in.'

'It's almost lunch-time,' protested Gemma.

'We'll make a start,' said Mr Miles, leading the way purposefully.

They worked in the sports store until the bell went for lunch – and then all the rest of the afternoon. Mr Miles drove them hard, and by half-past three they were all completely exhausted. But he had no chance to start digging up the floor because there were still broken bricks to take out. Tim heard Mr Wenlock saying: 'I didn't quite understand this morning's digging – or why you need—'

Mr Miles interrupted him crossly. 'I'm testing the sub-soil. It's a Council regulation.' Mr Wenlock looked doubtful but didn't seem able to think of a suitable reply.

There was an uneasy silence and then Tim piped up: 'Mr Miles?'

'Yes?' he snapped.

'I found this yesterday – in that pile of muck behind the bike sheds.'

Mr Miles took the key and stared at it. Then his face broke into a smile of such intense joy that even the level-headed Tim backed away.

'Good boy,' he muttered. 'That's really wonderful. You *are* a good boy. Wonderful . . .'

As they waited in the queue to be shown across the road Chris said, 'Why did you have to go and do that – go and give him that key?'

'Finders isn't keepers,' replied Tim, deliberately winding him up.

Chris ignored him. 'Did you see his face?' he persisted.

'He seemed pleased.'

'*Pleased?* He looked as if he'd won the pools.'

'Who's talking?' Miss Sands' voice rang out in the playground.

They said no more, standing as silently and wearily as the other children. Then they heard the ringing tones of Mrs Edge:

''Allo, 'allo, 'allo – what have we here? A bunch of sleep-walkers?' She screeched with laughter. 'You *have* been working hard.'

As they crossed the road, they saw Mr Ransom. He was looking even more death-like than before.

'Here we are – a bunch of real sleepy-heads. You won't be having any trouble with this lot, Ernest. They're all too tired to say a word,' chattered Mrs Edge.

'That's good, Marietta. They know what'll happen if they do.'

He drove them home at top speed and no one even tried to talk. In fact most of the children fell

asleep and Mr Ransom had to keep yelling at them every time he stopped the bus.

'Help each other to keep awake,' he hissed. 'You'll be left on the bus if you don't.'

'He's never satisfied, is he?' whispered Chris. 'How can we keep each other awake if we're not allowed to talk.' And of course he was heard although he was right down the end of the bus and well out of earshot.

When the bus stopped at the top of Chris and Tim's estate, Mr Ransom got out. He often went into the little corner shop to buy the lemon sherberts that he kept on the dashboard to give to the children when any of them seemed upset. As they passed his driving seat Chris saw the broken key, half-covered by a newspaper. Like lightning he picked it up and shoved it in his pocket.

Tim lay on his bed. He had just woken up. Looking at his watch he saw that it was after five. He had come in, just managed to eat his tea and then collapsed in his room.

'Tim.'

'Yes, Mum?'

She was shouting up the stairs. 'That Chris is

on the phone.' She always called him *that* Chris – to show her disapproval.

Somehow Tim dragged himself downstairs.

'What's up?'

'The library's open late tonight.' Chris's voice was tense with excitement.

'So what?'

'You coming?'

'Why should I?'

'I want to look something up.'

'Is that why you phoned – just to tell me the library's open?' Tim was indignant.

'Listen, you idiot. Do you want to solve the mystery or not?'

'What mystery?'

'The *school* mystery.'

'What school mystery?'

'You dim or something? Remember the newspaper cutting I showed you? I want to know more about the Abbey – more about where the well might be. More about the Masked Monks.'

'Look, Chris—'

'What's the matter with you?' asked Chris angrily. 'Why don't you wake up? How can Ransom hear what we're saying when we're right up the back of the bus? He must have X-ray hearing. And why did Sands know we'd been talking before he told her? What about all this clearing up? What are they searching for? And why can't I remember what happened in the boiler-house?' His voice ended on a kind of wail. 'They're magic, that lot. Black Magic.'

'You're barmy,' said Tim woodenly.

'All right. I'll go on my own. See you.'

'Hang on—'

'What then?'

'I'll come. But I still think you're barmy.'

Mrs Benfleet was a brilliant librarian and was always thinking up new ways of making the children's library fun.

'Hallo, you two,' she said.

'We're doing a school project,' said Chris. 'And we wondered if you could help us.'

'What's Miss Sands been thinking up now? She has such good ideas.'

'It's about the new school,' said Tim, looking rather uncomfortable.

'Or at least about what was there before it got built,' cut in Chris.

'That's easy,' said Mrs Benfleet. 'I'm surprised Miss Sands didn't tell you. It was Kelsinor –

Kelsinor Abbey. The Black Abbey they used to call it. It got burnt down in the eleventh century and – well, didn't you read the local paper?'

A chill of excitement swept through Chris. 'Yes, I just wanted to see if it was true – if there was any more on it.'

'There's a book in Old Stock you could go and have a look at. I think it's called *The Legend of Kelsinor*. Funny thing though—'

'What's that?' they chorused.

'Someone else has just asked to have a look at it. A gentleman.'

The sign was faded and pointed down a long winding corridor in the basement of the building. It actually read OLD STOCK but could have read TO THE DUNGEONS, for that's what the cobwebby passage looked like.

'Come *on*,' urged Chris.

'It looks spooky.' Tim hesitated.

'It's only the *library*.'

Reluctantly Tim followed Chris into the gloom. There was a musty smell now and neither of the boys would have been surprised if they had heard the dripping of water or even muffled screams.

Eventually the dusty corridor widened out into a room like a cavern, with rows of dingy-looking books in steel cabinets. A dim light bulb gleamed from the ceiling and the musty smell was stronger.

'This must be Old Stock,' whispered Tim shivering. He felt as if he was taking part in one of those old horror movies on television.

'She said Rack 6, Shelf B.'

'It's over here.'

There were long gloomy avenues between the shelves and the boys started towards the one they wanted. Suddenly they saw a shadow. And it was moving.

'It's Ransom.'

He was standing there, leaning against the shelving with an enormous book in his hands. It was bound in cracked leather that looked as if it was falling to pieces. For a few seconds Mr Ransom continued reading. Then he whirled round on them before they had a chance to run.

'I've been waiting for you two,' he hissed.

'Er—' began Chris, wondering again why Mr Ransom, who had driven them all on the school bus for years, should now seem so sinister.

'You took my key. Give it back. Now.'

But Chris was determined not to be bullied. 'Tim gave it to Mr Miles. Didn't you, Tim?'

'Yes—'

'And took it back again off the bus dashboard.'

'I did *not*.' Tim turned to Chris. 'Did I?'

'No,' said Chris firmly.

'But *you* did, didn't you?' said Mr Ransom, lunging at Chris and grabbing him by the neck of his T-shirt.

'Leave him alone,' yelled Tim, amazed that Mr Ransom could behave like this.

'That's right – leave me alone,' shouted Chris.

'No one will hear you down here. You're in Old Stock,' Mr Ransom gloated. His pale face seemed

to glow in the gloom. 'Now give me the key.'

'No.'

'So you admit you've got it then!'

'No.' Chris kicked him as hard as he could on the shins and Mr Ransom released his hold. Chris ran off, deeper and deeper into Old Stock, but Mr Ransom was after him in a few seconds with Tim just behind.

They ran through the space between the shelves, which seemed to get narrower and narrower. Chris came to a dead end and stood, his back against the wall, watching Mr Ransom gaining on him.

'Stop!' shouted Tim, but Mr Ransom ran on, his long thin form becoming fainter in the gloom. Tim picked out a book and flung it, then another and another. They rained down on Mr Ransom but he ran on, nearing Chris all the time. Then, in desperation, Tim made one last dash and rugby-tackled him. They both went down in a hail of flying books.

There was something brittle and twig-like about Mr Ransom and Tim rolled away from him in disgust. Ransom stumbled to his feet and pointed a finger at Chris. To Chris's amazement a tiny flare of fire curled from under Mr Ransom's nail. It leapt out with a sizzling snarl and Chris suddenly flushed a bright red. A great fiery wind seemed to seize him and he felt himself soaring up until he bashed his head on the ceiling. Slowly, he found himself turning upside down with the great hot wind above and below him.

Helplessly, Tim watched all this happening. He couldn't believe what he was seeing; it was like something out of Chris's vivid imagination. Then, Tim saw the contents of Chris's pockets falling on

to the floor: a penknife, some money, chewing-gum, aniseed balls, fluff, a fossil – and the key.

'Ah-hah!' Mr Ransom hooted in triumph and picked it up, leaving Chris upside-down, purple in the face.

Tim rushed forward and grabbed his hands, but it was no good, Chris was stuck in mid-air.

'You want him down?' hissed Mr Ransom.

'Yes,' pleaded Tim.

'I'm going to be sick,' pronounced Chris. 'All over both of you,' he added.

'We can't have that,' said Mr Ransom quickly,

sounding more like his old self – as he did if someone on the bus said they felt ill.

Chris began to turn the right way up again and then descend to the floor. He stood there panting while Mr Ransom pocketed the key.

'Now listen, you two. Keep out of this. Just keep out of this and you'll be all right.' But his voice was peculiar. It was as if there were two voices trying to speak at once – one, Mr Ransom's own voice, and the other, his new hissing way of speaking.

'Mr Ransom,' began Tim. 'What *is* going on? We only want to sort this out. Find out what . . .' He choked and broke off. There was an awful smell of boiling tar.

'Look,' said Chris. 'Look up there! It looks like – I remember now. It's Amanda's demon!'

The demon was about three foot high, coloured an angry red and sitting cross-legged on the edge of one of the high shelves.

'I saw him in the boiler-house. Goodness knows what Miss Holroyd saw. She certainly did a lot of screaming.' He turned to Tim. 'Can *you* see him?'

'Yes,' said Tim slowly. 'I can see him.'

The demon winked at them cheekily. He seemed to be quite at home.

45

'Kneel,' he said in a gravelly voice. 'Look at him – he's kneeling.'

Mr Ransom certainly was kneeling, his long thin figure hunched on the floor. Tim felt quite sorry for him now; he looked so pathetic.

'Kneel,' commanded the demon again.

'No way!' said Tim firmly, and Chris, who had been sinking to his knees, rapidly stood up again.

The demon grinned. 'You've got a lot of courage,' he said with a hint of admiration. 'But you really are a nuisance. These are the hard facts. You have forced me to use up precious energy and appear to you because you—' he pointed his fat red little finger at Tim – 'are too full of common sense. And I can't have that. And you—' his finger was pointing at Chris this time – 'are too imaginative and ask too many questions. And I can't have that either. Together you are a great nuisance to me.'

'Are you warning us off?' said Tim, but Chris dug him in the ribs.

'Of course he is, you idiot. We'll have to get out of here.'

But Tim's curiosity was getting the better of him. He just stood there, blocking Chris's path and staring at the demon.

'Your friend's right. Of course I've come to warn you off. The mortals I've taken on seem to be making a right mess of things, like all mortals do. But they'll get there in the end – providing I can keep the power going and stop them worrying about red herrings. Keys indeed! What's a key got to do with a well?' He paused and shook his head. Then his little red eyes became sharper. 'So stop interfering or I'll turn you both into ghouls.'

Appalled, Chris tried to push Tim down the dusty book-lined corridor.

'Are you the spirit of one of those masked monks?' Tim was saying. He sounded as if he was interviewing the demon for a project.

'Of course I'm not a masked monk!' said the demon indignantly. 'A right bunch of bungling mortals they were. I trained them to build up a little nest egg for me and what did they do? They hid the money down a well and then burnt the Abbey to the ground. So what on earth happened to my legacy? Buried beneath the ruins, I suppose. I didn't care much at the time.' He chuckled. 'Building up the nest egg had been fun and I didn't need the money – then. But now I do need it – urgently.'

'Why specially now?' said Tim curiously. 'Why should a demon need money at all?'

'I think I know why,' said Chris slowly, his teeth chattering despite the heat.

'Think you know everything, don't you?' sneered the demon. 'Well, if you're so clever, tell him why.'

'Bribery,' said Chris briefly. 'You wouldn't be able to get people to work for you if you couldn't offer them anything.'

'Just a business arrangement,' agreed the demon. 'Nothing unusual about that.'

'But why do you specially need it now?' persisted Tim. 'Why not before? It's a long time since the eleventh century, isn't it?'

'Things are getting depressingly better in the world today. It's really been pleasingly dreadful up to now. But now there's so much unexpected improvement, much better friendships between the nations. It makes me feel quite low. I shall *need* the money soon – to stir things up a bit.'

As Tim and Chris stared at him in horror the demon suddenly grew fainter.

'Now look what's happened. You've kept me here, with all your silly questions, and I'm losing power.' There was a flash, a strong smell of tar and a sudden stillness. The demon had gone.

Chris and Tim walked home, trying to work out what they were going to do. They had passed Mr Ransom kneeling in the corridor in a kind of trance. He made no attempt to stop them, but they hadn't dared to stay and read the book.

'Where do you think the well could be?' Chris was bubbling over with questions and ideas again. But Tim was exhausted, dazed by their encounter with the demon, and there was a nasty tingling sensation running up and down his spine.

'It's probably been built over,' he said wearily. 'I'll tell you something, though. My uncle's a builder – and he knows the foreman who was on the school site.'

'You mean – he might know where the well is?'

'He might know *something*.'

'Won't Miss Sands think of that?'

'She might. Eventually. We should try and get there first.'

'Yes, lads?'

The big man stood at his back door, pipe in hand. Tim's uncle had given them the address and they were both desperate to find out what they could.

'You're good at making things up, aren't you?' Tim had said to Chris.

'Not bad,' Chris had replied modestly. But now, faced with this suspicious-looking man, he had nothing much to say and Tim was stuck with doing all the talking.

'I'm sorry to bother you,' said Tim very politely. 'But my uncle, Bob Shepherd, said we should come and see you.'

'Good old Bob – he's a mate of mine.'

'Yes.' Tim began to feel more confident. 'You see – Chris and I are at St Elmer's and we're doing a school project on Kelsinor Abbey—'

'The Black Abbey and the Masked Monks?' He gave a great booming laugh. 'They were a right bunch that lot.'

'Yes. Anyway, someone said there might be an old well—'

'There is. We found it when we were putting up the bike sheds. But the archaeological society came down to have a look and they said it was sixteenth century.'

'Couldn't it have been on the site of an older well?'

'Could've been. You hoping there's treasure? Like the story?'

'Well—'

'Yes,' butted in Chris excitedly.

'Well, there ain't nothing there. They had instruments like, and they put them down – and there's nothing.'

'Where is the well?' asked Tim.

'It's covered by rubble – just by the bike sheds. We meant to cart it away – but had no time. Got called out on another job and—'

'Thank you,' said Tim, interrupting him. 'Thank you very much.'

Miss Sands stood on the platform with Miss Holroyd. She looked tense and worried, very far from her usual jolly self. But it was Miss Holroyd who spoke, quietly and doubtfully, as if she had been told what to say and didn't agree with it.

'Well, children, I should like to congratulate you all on doing a really wonderful job of clearing up our lovely school. All those odd corners, nooks and crannies—'

Miss Sands coughed loudly and Miss Holroyd hurried on. Tim noticed that Mr Miles had come in and was standing at the back of the hall, his eyes on her.

'And now I am going to call on Miss Sands to tell you about a new subject on our time-table.' She smiled in a painful sort of way. But before she could say any more Miss Sands stepped forward, her high heels tapping on the floor.

'Water divining,' she said. 'That is our new subject. Could you show us please, Mr Miles.'

Mr Miles walked up the aisle, a hazel branch

in his hand. 'Now look here. This is a hazel branch, this is. And each of you is going to get one. Don't break 'em – don't lose 'em – or you'll be in real trouble.'

Miss Sands coughed again and quickly interrupted him. 'Thank you very much, Mr Miles. Now children, this will be great fun. Back to normal lessons today, but at break-time and lunch-time we'll be doing this new subject. You can keep to yesterday's groups and each group'll take a section of the school. If anyone's twig starts bending you'll know you've found water. If that happens go and tell a teacher. All right?'

'Please, miss,' said Billy Pierce. 'What do you mean – bends?'

'Well, quivers, Billy. Moves.'

'Moves, miss?'

'Yes, moves. On its own.'

'On its *own*, miss?' said Amanda in surprise. 'How could it move on its own?'

'Never mind *how*,' said Miss Sands quickly. 'Just come and tell me if it *does*.'

'They're on to it,' whispered Chris to Tim in class. 'They're bound to find it.'

'Maybe the sticks won't work.'

'I bet one of them will.'

'So what can we do?'

Chris looked out of the window. The bright blue of the sky was being replaced by grey rain clouds. 'Nothing. The weather's going to do it for us.'

The rain lashed down and one of the teachers told them they wouldn't be doing any water-divining this morning – it was too wet already. At break, the boys stood in the shelter of the bike sheds.

54

They were just about to leave when Chris heard something. It was a kind of hollow drumming.

'Tim.'

'What?'

'Listen,' said Chris. 'Just listen.'

'I can't hear anything.'

'No?'

'Well – a sort of drumming sound.'

'Hollow drumming?' said Chris in an agony of impatience.

'Well – could be.'

'It *is*. Look.'

They both stared down at the compacted earth and cinder floor of the bike shed. The rain was hitting something certainly and they both began to scrape away at the muck. Gradually an outline began to form and then a circular wooden hatch.

'I'm sure this is it,' panted Chris. 'The foreman said the later one's outside and the old one could be near it.'

The bell sounded. 'We've got to go,' said Tim.

'Cover it up again,' said Chris in a panic. They scrabbled earth over it and ran back to the school. Soaked and filthy, they darted into the boys' toilet, trying to clean themselves up and scrub the mud out from under their nails. But before they could do anything they saw Mr Miles emerging from one of the toilets with a bucket and mop.

'What have you two been up to?' he asked suspiciously.

'Nothing.'

'You're filthy.'

'We were mucking about,' said Chris feebly.

'Look at your nails. You been digging in the earth?'

'No,' replied Tim.

'You hang on here.'

'Why?'

'I'm fetching Miss Sands. That's why.'

'We'll be late for class.'

'Stay where you are.'

They stayed, miserably waiting for Miss Sands. Suddenly Chris shivered.

'You scared?'

'No. It's just – she used to be good fun. I know she was strict but we all liked her, didn't we? And now—' The chill was with him again. 'I *am* scared,' he muttered.

'Yes,' said Tim. 'She used to be OK really. That wretched demon's changed everything.'

She was not long in coming, and when she did

Miss Sands looked thunderous. Her chins wobbled and her face was brick red.

'Mr Miles tells me you've been digging in the dirt.'

'No—' said Chris. 'We weren't really.'

'Show me your nails.'

Miserably they held them up.

'What rubbish – they're filthy. Tell me what you were doing immediately or I'll have to give you the cane.'

'There's no beating in this school,' Tim reminded her angrily.

'Things can change,' she snapped. 'Now, tell me what you've been up to.'

Tim had a brilliant idea. 'Actually,' he said, 'actually, we've been trying to clear out the rain barrel.'

Chris stared at him as if he had gone crazy, but although Miss Sands looked at him suspiciously, Tim went on quite confidently.

'It's all clogged up with builders' rubble. We thought we'd clear all the muck out so it can take in water again. Then Mr Miles can fill his watering can from it – like he used to at the old school.'

'You were not dressed for clearing out a rain barrel,' said Miss Sands sharply. 'You should have been wearing your craft aprons.'

'We're sorry,' said Chris, anxious to play his part. 'We didn't think.'

'We only wanted to help,' put in Tim. 'We liked that clearing out. We wanted to do some more.'

Miss Sands's face was working. There came a knock at the door.

'Hallo there.' It was the paper-thin voice of Mr Ransom. Immediately the boys exchanged anxious glances.

'Yes?' Miss Sands turned to open the door.

'I was looking for you, Miss Sands. But I certainly didn't expect to find you here.'

Miss Sands looked very embarrassed. 'I was

telling off these two boys for being so filthy,' she said quickly. 'They claim to have emptied the rain barrel in the playground.'

'We didn't empty it,' said Chris. 'We just made a start.'

'I really needed to speak to you about some changes in the bus times, but I'll go and look.' Mr Ransom glided away and they remained with Miss Sands, locked in painful silence.

After what seemed like a very long time, Mr Ransom returned. There was a grim smile on his white face. 'Not been touched,' he hissed triumphantly. 'What you two been up to then?'

'I told you,' said Tim desperately. 'We've only just started.'

'Not been touched,' Mr Ransom repeated.

'What is the meaning of this?' asked Miss Sands.

'We've just been scratching the surface of it. We thought it would be a nice surprise for Mr Miles.'

'Come to my study,' said Miss Sands.

'Bend over.'

The study looked different. All the pictures had been taken down, a mirror had been removed

59

from the wall and a fire burned brightly in the grate, despite the fact that the weather was still summery. The flames were fierce and Tim wondered why she wanted it so hot. Then he remembered the boiler-house. Maybe heat kept up the power?

Both Tim and Chris were determined they were not going to be beaten.

'It's against the rules,' said Chris. 'You've always been against it. You said so.'

'Things have changed. You're still interfering. You must be punished.'

'No,' said Tim. 'Call Miss Holroyd. She'll remind you – tell you that you're not allowed to beat us.'

'I have no intention of calling Miss Holroyd. *I* am still in charge round here. Now if you tell me what you were *really* doing I may be lenient.'

'We've told you what we were doing,' yelled Chris. 'That's all we *can* do.'

'Bend over, Timothy.' She started to search the room for something to hit him with. Chris dashed outside. Miss Holroyd should be in her classroom, he thought, and he would summon her to their aid. She wouldn't let them be beaten.

'Come back instantly,' boomed Miss Sands, but

Chris was already half-way down the corridor when he spotted a big vase full of roses. The idea darted into his head immediately. If she liked heat so much – how would she react to cold water? He'd cool her off and maybe allow Tim to escape. Chris picked up the vase, took out the roses, and rushed back to Miss Sands' room.

'Take that,' shouted Chris and threw the water all over her. There was the most amazing reaction. For a moment Miss Sands literally seemed to shrivel, to become smaller, with her skin all puckered up. As for her chins, they looked as if they were going to dissolve. Then, wiping away the water, Miss Sands shrieked:

'You devil. You little devil.' She pushed Tim aside and came after Chris. Devil, thought Chris. You can talk! He dodged her and ran straight into the arms of Miss Holroyd who stared at Miss Sands in horror.

'What are you doing?'

'Punishing these boys. One of them has just assaulted me.' But Miss Holroyd's eyes were fixed on her raised arm.

'My dear Miss Sands – Emily. You are still not yourself.' As she spoke, Miss Holroyd seemed to gain in stature and confidence. 'You must come and lie down,' she said calmly.

'What?'

'You are not well. *I* will deal with these wretched—'

'Augustina – I must remind you *I* am in charge of discipline in this school.'

'My dear Emily—'

'My dear Augustina—'

They stood, locked eyeball to eyeball. Miss Sands was the first to break. Maybe she was weakened by the water, thought Chris.

'Very well.' She shivered with anger as she

turned to Tim and Chris. 'You will write out "*I must not lie or throw water at my teachers*" two hundred times. Is that clear?'

'Yes, Miss Sands,' they chorused.

Miss Sands fixed Miss Holroyd with a beady glare. 'We must talk, Miss Holroyd.'

'By all means, Miss Sands.'

Miss Holroyd smiled bravely as Miss Sands left the room.

Chris and Tim were thinking the same thing. What would happen to poor, brave Miss Holroyd? The new Miss Sands was very formidable indeed.

That afternoon a hot September sun dried the rain and water-divining was organised. Then Chris had his great idea.

'I can fiddle this,' he said. 'And draw the fire.'

'What are you on about?' asked Tim. They were standing in the middle of the school playground, their hazel sticks in hand.

'All I have to do is to get it to work – do it myself.'

'All right, super-brain. Then one of the teachers takes over and you're proved a fake.'

'But they won't be able to,' he said.

'Why not?'

'Because I'm going to break the stick.'

Tim grinned. He had to admit that Chris was a quick thinker. Maybe it would work – or at least it would hold them off for a while. But then what were they going to do?

'Where shall we make the find?'

'What about over there?' Chris pointed to the new flower-beds that had been dug at the front of the school. There was nothing in them – just mounds of earth. Holding their sticks out in front of them, they walked towards the beds, just as over a hundred children were doing around them. All they could hope was that no one had reached the bike sheds yet.

'Now for it!' Chris began to jerk at his hazel stick until it was swinging wildly. Then Tim stopped him.

'What's up?'

'I just remembered something. They won't believe you. You're too suspicious. But if it was me—'

'You mean you're prepared to fiddle it?' Chris looked at him in amazement. 'I mean – you don't fiddle anything. Do you?'

'I do in a good cause,' said Tim.

* * *

Miss Sands was first on the scene as Tim's shouts drew a crowd around him. Pushing her way through, she arrived triumphant and panting just as the hazel stick broke in two.

'It was going like mad,' he said.

She gave him a strange glance and grabbed another stick from a nearby child. Nothing happened. She took another. It gave a slight jerk. Suddenly a drop of rain hit Chris on the forehead and he knew they were saved, at least for the day. More drops followed until it was raining quite heavily.

Miss Sands looked up at the sky and waved her fist. A flash of lightning suddenly split the clouds and there was a tremendous roar of thunder. She was so scared that she fell backwards into the flower-bed.

Chris laughed before he could stop himself, for she looked like a stranded whale. As Tim leant forward to help her up, Mr Ransom pushed his way through the crowd and pulled her to her feet. Then she turned on Chris, for a moment looking hurt and upset.

'Did you laugh, Chris?'

'No, Miss Sands,' stammered Chris.

'But you did laugh, didn't you?' She sounded

rather angry now and Tim could see the sliver of blue fire at the end of her fingertip. Would she use it? he wondered.

Mr Ransom quickly took her hand. 'Come on, Emily,' he said. 'Let me help you to your room.' As he led her away he hissed at Tim and Chris, 'I'll fix you two – see if I don't.' He brushed past them and disappeared into the school. Then, as the crowd started to disperse, Miss Holroyd appeared.

'Are you two all right?' she asked. Tim felt a surge of hope for there was something in her eyes that told him she was an ally.

The rain was still streaking down as they went home that evening.

'You know what,' said Tim. 'We'll have to go and find that treasure – before they get to it.'

'When?' asked Chris reluctantly, knowing what he was going to say.

'Tonight. After midnight.'

'We'll get done for breaking and entering.'

'That's a risk we'll have to take.'

The night was soft and dark. A sickle moon shone over the bike sheds, making them look bigger and

more menacing than they really were. The boys had kept to the side streets, taking turns to carry a large spade.

Both were very nervous. Chris had hardly been able to bear the wait for Tim to throw dirt at his window. He had clambered out and somehow – with amazing good fortune – no one had stopped them on their journey. And here they were, at a quarter to one, standing at the entrance to St Elmer's.

Once inside, they made for the bike sheds and began to dig. It was very hard work and they took turns, working for what seemed like hours. Then, when the first grey streak of dawn appeared in the sky, Chris's spade struck something metallic. The sound seemed to ring out deafeningly.

Cautiously they looked round but the night was very still. A dog barked somewhere a long way off and a light wind stirred the dusty-looking elm trees at the edge of the school grounds. Tim knelt down and began to scratch at the surface with the spade. They had no torch and could hardly see what they were doing.

'I think it's a kind of – chest.'

It took them another back-breaking half-hour of digging until they managed to uncover it. The chest was rusty and parts of it were falling away.

'What do we do with it?' hissed Tim. 'It's too big to carry home.'

'I know,' said Chris. 'Let's bung it in the pump house of the new swimming-pool.'

'They'll soon find it there.'

'We'll get Miss Holroyd to ring the police first thing in the morning.'

'It *is* first thing in the morning,' said Tim gloomily, looking up at the lightening sky. 'Stay here and I'll see if the coast is clear.'

'Don't leave me,' wailed Chris.

'I'll be back in a minute.' Tim stole away into the blackness, leaving Chris gazing around him. Every shadow seemed to have eyes.

Tim looked round the playground. The moonlight seemed to pick out strange shapes but there was no one there. Then he saw the light in the boiler-house. It was flickering. Flickering like flames. He ducked down behind the big dustbins and waited, not daring to move. After a while, thinking of Chris, he stood up and then ducked down again very quickly. Someone was entering the playground.

Chris was very agitated. Had Tim been kidnapped? Taken to the boiler-house? Roasted? Become a demon? Were they even now marching across the playground to get him? The shadows danced in the breeze, and when Chris looked up at the pale moon, he thought he saw it wink.

Mrs Edge scurried across the playground, heading for the boiler-house. She stopped, knocked on the door and it quickly opened. Tim could feel the heat of the flames which seemed to send licking, darting tongues out of the door. Then Mrs Edge vanished inside.

Suddenly, Tim felt so curious that he couldn't bear it. He *had* to see what was going on in the boiler-house – whatever the danger. His mind made up, he tiptoed across the playground until he was standing right by the window.

It was no good, Chris could no longer bear night life in the bike sheds and he was desperate to see where Tim had gone. He cautiously walked out into the playground. To his horror, Tim was nowhere to be seen. Then he spotted him, crouched down by the boiler-house. He was about to run to join him when Chris felt something bony on his neck. And before he could cry out, a hand closed over his mouth.

'What are you doing here?' said Mr Ransom.

'Nothing,' grunted Chris.

'Don't be absurd, boy.'

'Let go.'

'What are you—'

In desperation, Chris kicked out behind him and Mr Ransom gave a grunt of pain. He kicked again, the hand came away and Mr Ransom

lurched backwards, hitting his head on an over-loaded dustbin with a dull thud. He lay on the ground, rolling his eyes. When Chris looked into them he could see – or thought he could see – miniature tongues of flame. Then Mr Ransom's eyes closed and he went limp.

Knowing he hadn't long, Chris dashed silently across to Tim, who was still peering fixedly into the window as if someone had hypnotised him.

'Listen, Ransom got me and – what's the matter?'

He *was* hypnotised. Tim was chanting some-thing under his breath. Gradually it was becoming a whisper. 'Kelsinor,' Tim whispered. 'Kelsinor.'

Terrified, Chris looked through the window. Mrs Edge was there in her white coat, sitting on an orange-box, warming her hands at the boiler. Miss Sands and Mr Miles were hunched in front of the boiler too, but there was no sign of the demon.

'Tim!' Chris grabbed at him but was shaken off. 'Tim!' He was shaken off again. Then, to his horror, Chris saw that Tim was struggling to his feet, one hand poised to knock at the door. Again he grabbed him but Tim just pushed him away. In desperation Chris punched him in the back as hard as he could. Tim turned round.

'What'd you do that for?' He blinked several times and the funny look went out of his eyes.

'Ssh.'

'Eh?'

'We're outside the boiler-house. You got hyp-notised somehow.'

'I did feel funny.'

'We can't stay here – someone will come. Besides, I knocked out Ransom.'

'You what?' Tim was horrified.

'Well, he slipped really. Anyway, he's lying on the ground with his eyes closed and we've got to

73

get the chest into the pump house. Now.'

'OK.'

Tim seemed fully recovered and they both ran back the way they had come. But when they reached the spot where Mr Ransom had been lying there was no one to be seen.

'He's got it,' said Chris miserably. 'He must have found the chest.'

'Who says?' snapped Tim. 'Let's go and see.'

They crept back to the bike sheds, fearful that at any moment Mr Ransom would jump out at them. But there was no sign of him and the chest remained where it was, battered and earthy. Warily, Tim and Chris walked towards it.

Puffing and panting, thinking they were going to be caught at any moment, they staggered across the playground with the chest between them. They could still see the flickering flames in the boiler-house but they seemed less fierce. They made it to the swimming pool and humped their load over the fence.

'Mrs Edge will hear us,' said Tim in a panic.

They waited, listening, but nothing happened. There was still no sign of Mr Ransom and the boiler-house door remained firmly closed.

'What do you think they're doing now?' said Tim as he helped push the chest into the narrow space inside the pump house.

'Maybe they're dancing in the flames,' replied Chris. 'I reckon they're pretty occupied. It's Ransom I'm worrying about.'

They tiptoed back across the playground to the bike sheds and scrambled over the wall, dropping to the pavement as cautiously as they could.

'I feel as if he's watching us,' said Tim. 'Watching us and biding his time.'

'For what?'

'Tomorrow.'

'Don't let's go in, then.'

'We've got to.'

'Why?' Chris was tired and he felt sleepy and stupid.

'Because we've got to get the chest to Miss Holroyd.'

'S'pose it's empty?'

'It was heavy, you prat.'

'We should have wrenched it open.'

'How? We had no time.'

'We should—'

'Don't start arguing now.'

'I can't go in,' wailed Chris. 'They'll be waiting for us. I'm sure they're setting a trap.'

'So we'll come prepared.'

'How?'

Tim thought for a minute. 'Water-pistols,' he said suddenly.

'You gone barmy?'

'No. Remember what happened in Miss Sands' study?'

'She sort of . . . withered up.'

'Yes,' said Tim. 'I reckon something very nasty happens to that lot when they get wet.'

'You think they'll attack?'

Tim nodded. 'We've got what they want. And they'll soon find out.'

'If they stop dancing long enough,' said Chris with a slight smile. 'What about Ransom though?'

'Maybe he's still concussed – staggering about somewhere.'

'Let's hope he doesn't come to yet,' replied Chris as they began to run through the darkened streets.

4 . . . *Thursday*

A few hours later, Tim and Chris waited nervously for the school bus. But when it came Mr Ransom was at the wheel as usual and showed no sign of being anything other than his new bad-tempered self.

'You look tired,' whispered Amanda to Tim.

'Silence,' said Mr Ransom. 'Absolute silence.'

'What's up?' mouthed Billy. But Mr Ransom even seemed to sense that.

'Be quiet,' he hissed, and they were.

'Miss Holroyd.'

'I'm very busy, Tim.'

'We want to speak to you.'

'What is it?' She peered at them anxiously.

'We want to speak to you in your room. Alone.'

Miss Holroyd stared at them for a moment and then bustled forward. She seemed to lack her new strength today and looked old and tired. She led them into her room and said sharply: 'Well?'

'We've found what they're looking for.'

'They?'

'Miss Sands and Mrs Edge and Mr Ransom and Mr Miles – they've been taken over by a demon.'

'Is this some kind of silly joke?'

'No,' said Tim slowly. 'You must know the school's been built on the site of the Black Abbey – you must know about the Masked Monks.'

'Oh, that silly old story—'

'It's true,' said Tim quietly. 'There's a demon and he's taken over Miss Sands and the others. He's making them look for the treasure, and when they get it they're going to—'

'We found it,' interrupted Chris. 'We dug it up.'

'You did *what*?'

'We dug it up.'

'You dug—' She was staring wildly at them and her glasses were all steamed up.

'Come and see,' said Tim.

Numbly but obediently, Miss Holroyd followed them out of her room and down the corridor.

'Where are we going?' she asked.

'Ssh,' said Tim. 'They'll hear.'

Miss Holroyd gazed at him blankly, but just then Mr Miles came out of Miss Sands' office.

'Miss Holroyd, could you spare me a minute?'

'I'm a little busy at the moment.'

'It's rather urgent—'

'In a *moment*, Mr Miles.'

Tim fingered the water-pistol in his pocket. It was the biggest he had and it was loaded to the brim. He looked at Chris and guessed he was doing the same. They both knew it would not be long before they would have to defend themselves.

'Well?'

It was still there in the pump house. Tim and Chris both breathed heavy sighs of relief.

'What a curious chest.'

'It's the Masked Monks' loot – what they got from robbing people,' said Chris.

'The who?' She was staring down at it. Then she said very quietly: 'Someone seems to have forced the lock.'

In fact the chest was a little open and when Tim rushed over to it and opened the lid, he yelled: 'It's empty. They've beaten us to it!'

They gazed at it, horrified, until they were interrupted by a sudden cackle of wild laughter. All three turned to see Mrs Edge standing on the threshold. 'Playing hide-and-seek, are we?'

'No,' said Miss Holroyd coldly.

'Hunt the treasure then?' She gave one of her piercing shrieks of laughter.

'I don't know what you're talking about.'

'Oh yes you do,' said Mrs Edge.

Furious, they stared at each other in silence then Miss Holroyd rapped out: 'I don't know what you're doing here at this time of day, Mrs Edge. We don't expect you until three-fifteen.'

'And *we* don't expect you to interfere,' said Mrs Edge sharply. 'Why don't you mind your own business? Why don't you *all* mind your own business?'

'How dare you?'

'I could tell you a thing or two about these naughty boys,' said Mrs Edge. 'They've been digging for treasure trove. Treasure that doesn't belong to them. The Kelsinor treasure. And apart from that – which is quite bad enough – they've been hurting Mr Ransom.'

'Hurting him?'

'Knocked him out they did and ran home. But he was watching. We don't have full powers, we can't see everything. But we soon will. And the treasure belonged to the Abbey. To the Monks. And now it belongs to us.'

'It does *not*,' yelled Tim. 'It belongs to the Queen or something.'

'We'll give it to the police,' said Chris.

'If valuables have been found—' put in Miss Holroyd.

Mrs Edge cackled with uproarious laughter. 'Of course they've been found. And we'll be using them for a very good cause.'

'Cause?' Miss Holroyd stared at her with deep suspicion.

'We need funds, you see. Funds for our

activities.'

'I'm sure your activities are illegal,' said Miss Holroyd severely.

Ignoring her, Mrs Edge looked at her watch. 'It's time for assembly. Miss Sands requires your presence.'

'Where's the treasure?' shouted Tim. 'Where have you hidden it?'

'That would be telling,' teased Mrs Edge.

Instantly Chris whipped out his water-pistol. 'Tell me or I fire.'

'What's that?' For the first time she looked frightened. 'Put it down.'

'It's a water pistol.'

'Water!' she shrieked.

'The liquid you don't like,' smiled Tim, getting his own out. 'It's our turn to laugh now.'

'Put those – things – down!' screamed Mrs Edge.

'Where's the treasure?'

'I wouldn't dream of—'

'Where's the treasure?' repeated Chris threateningly.

'I tell you—'

'Take this then.' He squirted a jet of water which narrowly missed her.

'No more,' she pleaded.

'Tell.'

'The others will—'

'Tell!' He fired, once again deliberately missing her. She reeled back.

'All right, I'll tell. But you'll never get it.'

'Why not?' threatened Tim.

'Because Mr Miles has it in the boiler-house – and you'd never go in there.'

'Why not?'

'Because it's our world.'

'The boiler-house belongs to the Education Authority,' interrupted Miss Holroyd. 'How dare you claim it as your own.'

'Let's go,' said Tim.

'Where?' asked Chris.

'To the boiler-house. We've got a hostage, haven't we?'

The playground was empty as they crossed it. They made a strange procession: Mrs Edge with her hands above her head, Chris and Tim with their water-pistols levelled at her back and Miss Holroyd following along behind.

'You have exceeded your duty, Mrs Edge,' she was telling her. 'You have *all* exceeded your duties.'

'Ssh,' said Tim.

'Don't shush me, Timothy.'

'We don't want the others coming out.'

Miss Holroyd suddenly went quiet but it was too late.

'Stop!' Miss Sands was standing outside the assembly hall. From behind her came the sound of children singing. She looked grim.

'Move it,' said Tim to Mrs Edge. 'Or you'll get splattered.' He turned to Chris. 'Take Sands!'

With a trembling hand, Chris turned his water-pistol on Miss Sands. This isn't going to be so easy, he thought. For a wild moment he saw himself as a cowboy. Gun-fight at the OK Corral.

'Give me that at once, Christopher.' She turned to Miss Holroyd. 'Augustina, what are you doing?'

'Stay where you are—' said Chris.

'Give me that water-pistol at once.'

'I'll fire.'

'You wouldn't dare.'

Suddenly Miss Sands grabbed a dustbin lid. Chris fired but she was quick, despite her size, and she bore down on him, using the lid as a shield. Then, just as she was nearing Chris, Tim pulled open the boiler-house door, still covering

Mrs Edge as he did so. That was a big mistake.
The heat was so fierce that he staggered back.
With a cry of joy Mrs Edge rushed forward and
slammed the door behind her.

'This is outrageous,' said Miss Holroyd suddenly. She turned to Miss Sands. 'Put that dustbin
lid down, Emily. I demand an explanation. Have
you taken leave of your senses? You've been acting
most strangely recently.'

But Miss Sands wasn't listening. Instead she
was still advancing on Chris. Terrified, he shot
his water-pistol high in the air and she fell down,

the dustbin lid rolling away from her. He was just about to fire again when the boiler-house door was thrown open. There was a rush of searing heat and Mr Ransom stood there, hunched in a huge mac. Tim shot at him desperately but Mr Ransom grabbed him, dragged him into the boiler-house and slammed the door before Chris could do anything.

'This is outrageous,' shrilled Miss Holroyd.

'This is it,' hissed Mr Ransom. 'You're for it now.'

Tim was almost overcome by the heat. The place was red hot and yet the doors of the boiler itself were open wide and he could see they were quite clean. This time there was no fire in the boiler at all. Then he spotted Mr Miles, sitting astride one of the central heating pipes. He had a bag of gold coins in his hand and next to him was a giggling Mrs Edge.

'Come here, Timothy,' said Mr Ransom.

Tim shuddered. But he still had the presence of mind to fire his water-pistol. Nothing happened and when he looked he saw to his horror that all the water had evaporated.

'Now you're *really* for it,' hissed Mr Ransom again, advancing on him.

'Don't move,' said Chris. He checked his pistol. There was still a fair amount of water in it. Miss Sands stopped and snakes of fire curled from her fingertips. But they didn't reach him. Meanwhile Miss Holroyd was struggling with the boiler-house door.

'You'll burn yourself,' he yelled.

But she had opened it and stood on the doorstep, the tongues of fire billowing around her.

'Mr Miles, Mrs Edge, Mr Ransom – unhand that child at once and come to your senses. You are behaving—' But the heat finally penetrated her anger and she fell back with a gasp. She gazed in distress at the terrified Chris, who was still holding Miss Sands at bay. 'There's only one thing for it,' muttered Miss Holroyd. 'I'm taking drastic action.'

'Don't leave me,' Chris wailed.

'Keep her at bay,' was all she said.

'Right,' said Mr Ransom, dragging Tim towards him. 'You're going to meet our master.'

'I've already met him,' said Tim desperately.

'Well, you're going to meet him again.'

Tim looked up and saw the little red demon,

sitting on top of the boiler. He had a mask in his hand and winked at Tim.

'I'm a Masked Monk now,' he said with a grin. 'They certainly stole a lot of money for me.'

'Treasure trove belongs to the Queen,' said Tim, trying to sound brave.

'You know too much,' he said. 'And you need punishment.'

'What are you going to do to me?' asked Tim, his whole body shaking with fright.

'You're going to become one of us.'

'How?'

'Well, it's not very pleasant,' said the demon with a smirk.

They all began to laugh. Their laughter sounded like the roaring of flames and the boiler-house was so hot Tim thought he would faint.

Suddenly the door was thrown open and Miss Holroyd stood there again, her face furious.

'You have all gone beyond your duties,' she said. 'You are forcing me to take action.'

Tim could see there was something in her hand, something that snaked out behind her. A hose.

Suddenly the boiler-house was transformed into spluttering, hissing steam as the hose flailed with water. Mrs Edge wept and screamed, Mr Miles

90

cursed, and Mr Ransom yelled with anger. Then, without warning, the hose stopped.

'Oh dear,' said Miss Holroyd. 'It must have come off the tap.'

'Chris'll fix it,' panted Tim. He went to the door to see him standing guard over Miss Sands. 'The hose has come off,' he yelled.

Chris sprinted off while Miss Sands staggered to her feet, glaring at Miss Holroyd.

'Augustina,' she said. 'You are interfering.'

'What are you doing playing about with the hose?' asked Mrs Small from the Reception Class.

'Miss Holroyd told me to turn it back on, miss. She's hosing down the boiler-house.'

'She's what?'

But Chris didn't want to waste time talking and he quickly reconnected the hose.

'It's OK,' he yelled at Tim.

'What's going on?' snapped Mrs Small.

'We're getting rid of a demon, miss,' said Chris as he ran off.

'How dare you speak to me like that!' shouted Mrs Small and made a grab for him. But she was too late.

* * *

'Now, Augustina.'

'Now, Emily.'

They were struggling for the nozzle of the hose when it suddenly burst into life again and Miss Holroyd directed the full force of the jet into the boiler-house.

The steam gradually became cooler and Tim saw the demon shivering on top of the boiler. He had his red arms wrapped round his stunted red body and was weeping hot tears of rage. Then he turned towards the pile of gold coins and jewels that glimmered in the corner of the boiler house. He stared at them but nothing happened. Then the demon turned back to Tim.

'I'll destroy you too,' he snarled and stared again. But all Tim felt was a blast of warm air.

'You've no power left,' said Tim with relief.

The jet from the hose caught the demon full in the chest and flattened him against the wall. Steam rose, there was a long wailing cry and then all that was left of him was a wet blob on the wall – and a small mask on the floor. Tim went over and picked it up. It would be quite a souvenir.

'Is there a fire, Miss Holroyd?' asked Mrs Small as she panted up.

'Yes, something caught alight. It's out now,' she said quietly.

'Well, I must say – what singular presence of mind.' She peered into the steam. As she did so, Miss Holroyd turned to Tim and Chris and put her finger to her lips. From the boiler-house trailed Mrs Edge, Mr Miles and Mr Ransom. They were soaked, dazed and utterly bewildered. Beside Miss Holroyd stood Miss Sands.

'What on earth has been going on, Augustina? I can't remember anything.'

'There was an explosion in the boiler-house,' said Miss Holroyd calmly. 'You must all be

94

suffering from shock.' She turned to Mrs Small. 'Our colleagues were so brave – they rushed ahead of me and were caught in the blast. But everything's all right.'

Miss Sands nodded and stumbled across to Mr Ransom. She put a hand on his shoulder and he shook his head, unable to understand what had happened. Mr Miles' arm was round Mrs Edge, who was sobbing quietly.

Miss Holroyd took Tim and Chris aside. 'I don't know what's been going on, but whatever has happened is over – and that's the way I want to keep it. Do you understand? Take that treasure down to the police station. I'll come with you.'

They both nodded and looked at the four adults who were asking each other in bewilderment what had occurred.

'They're themselves again,' said Chris. Then he turned to Miss Holroyd. 'Do you know, miss—'

'Do I know what, Christopher?'

'You're the bravest woman I've ever met, miss.'

'Thank you.' There was a sob in her voice. She went over to Miss Sands who was standing there, looking like a deflated barrage balloon, and put her arms round her.

* * *

Miss Holroyd stood on the stage, looking down at the assembled pupils.

'As you may know, the treasure of Kelsinor Abbey was found – under some rubble. The builders must have dug up the casket without realising what it was. I'd like to congratulate Timothy Shepherd and Christopher Elliott for – er – making the discovery. Naturally we took the casket to the police station and claimed treasure trove.' She smiled brightly at the excited children. 'And the good news is that we shall be getting a reward – a big donation to the school fund.'

During the outburst of spontaneous applause, Chris turned to Tim and said, 'Do you think the demon will ever come back?'

'He might.' Tim tapped the water-pistol in his pocket. 'But if he does – we'll be ready.'